I AM YOURS AND YOU ARE MINE
God's Love

I AM YOURS AND YOU ARE MINE

God's Love

Rev. Kelvin McKisic

I am Yours and You are Mine
Copyright © 2020 by Rev. Kelvin McKisic

Christian / Religion

Library of Congress Control Number: 2020910366
ISBN-13:   Paperback: 978-1-64749-145-1
              ePub: 978-1-64749-159-8

All rights reserved. No part of this publication may be reproduced, distributed, or transmitted in any form or by any means, including photocopying, recording, or other electronic or mechanical methods, without the prior written permission of the publisher or author, except in the case of brief quotations embodied in critical reviews and certain other noncommercial uses permitted by copyright law.

Although every precaution has been taken to verify the accuracy of the information contained herein, the author and publisher assume no responsibility for any errors or omissions. No liability is assumed for damages that may result from the use of information contained within.

Printed in the United States of America

GoToPublish LLC
1-888-337-1724
www.gotopublish.com
info@gotopublish.com

Table of Contents

Introduction ix
Beginning of God's Love 11
His Love Is Faithful 14
His Love Delivers 19
His Love Provides 25
In His Love Are Planned Provisions 30
His Longsuffering Love 33
His Love Forgives 37
His Love Flows with Compassion and Grace 40
In His Love We Are Cared For 42
His Love Brought Us Jesus 46
His Love Gives Us an Example to Live By 48
Healings Come from His Love 51
    By His Love Our Faith Brings Healing 53
By His Word We Are Healed 56
His Love Is Inseparable 58
His Love Does Not Forget 60
He Loved Us First 62
A Self-sacrificing Love 64
An Everlasting Love 66
We Are Saved by His Love 68
The Bible is Love 69
    Love Is the Highest 72
    God's Love Is a Perfect Love 73
    We Are Assured of His Love 74
    Love Is Not an Option 74
    Love Is the Way 75

You were created for me to love.
I will provide for you, I will support you in your times of need, and
I will hide you from all harms.

In me, you will find peace, joy, and ever-lasting life.

Love,
God

Introduction

Love is both an attribute of God and a description of his being. His love is unconditional, and he is the one who first loved us. God showed his love in the Garden of Eden when he removed Adam and Eve from the garden. He removed them from the garden so that they would not eat of the Tree of Life and live forever in the grip of sin. God's love abounds all around us, and he wants us to open our eyes to see how much he loves us.

"In the beginning God created the heaven and the earth."
Genesis 1:1

Beginning of God's Love

God created man in his own image and likeness and gave man dominion over the earth and all things that live on it. Then he blessed us. His love created us to be the very best; Psalm 139:14 states, *"I will praise thee; for I am fearfully and wonderfully made: marvellous are thy works; and that my soul knoweth right well."*

When sin entered the world through deception of the serpent, God made provisions for man to be saved from the disobedience of man in the garden. Through his love, he set in motion the birth of Jesus Christ, the light of the world and savior for all mankind. Although mankind was now cursed because of disobedience to God's command to not eat of the tree of the knowledge of good and evil, his love gave us an out from the effect of sin.

> *"And I will put enmity between thee and the woman, and between thy seed and her seed; it shall bruise thy head, and thou shalt bruise his heel."* Genesis 3:15

Jesus Christ is that seed! I say, "Is" because Jesus rose from the dead and ascended into heaven, still living to bring salvation to all who believe upon Him.

> *"For God so loved the world, that he gave his only begotten Son, that whosoever believeth in him should not perish, but have everlasting life."* John 3:16

God so loves us that he created a place for us to live before he created us. He created the world with all its animals, he created the garden, and he saw all that he had made, and it was good. After creating all the provisions for man, he then created man. He did not want man to wait for all the wonderful things he has for us; he created man last so that we would awake and see the wonders of our Father's hand. Through his love and grace, we can arise each day, so take the time to see and experience his love through his creations.

Look at yourself and see how wonderfully you are made. Our Father in heaven has made you and given you provisions to make it through your day. Look to him and be thankful, for in his love we find strength. Elijah the prophet experienced this awakening to find the provisions that God had prepared for him after Elijah fled in fear of Jezebel (1 Kings 19). In chapter 19 of 1 Kings, we find Elijah sitting under a tree praying to God that he has had enough and cannot continue. God heard his prayer and sent an angel to minister to him. Elijah awoke to see the provisions God had prepared for him—food that was ready for him to eat, to help him regain his strength and renew his courage to continue serving the Lord. Strengthened by the food, Elijah was able to travel for forty days and nights to the mountain of Horeb.

I AM YOURS AND YOU ARE MINE: GOD'S LOVE

"Even the youths shall faint and be weary, and the young men shall utterly fall: But they that wait upon the LORD shall renew their strength; they shall mount up with wings as eagles; they shall run, and not be weary; and they shall walk, and not faint."
Isaiah 40:30-31

His Love Is Faithful

Jesus gives us his word that he will never leave us or forsake us. That is a faithful saying in which love abounds. God has, throughout the ages, has been faithful to his promise of a better world for those who love him.

> *"And they that know thy name will put their trust in thee: for thou, LORD, hast not forsaken them that seek thee."* Psalm 9:10

We can rest assured that the Lord will care for us in his love, the love that caused him to create the world for us to live in it. God's love for us is revealed in his creation: being made in his likeness, we show the same kind of love that he shows us. In his likeness, we, as man and woman, love each other and love our children that result from a godly union. This unconditional love is not created by man, but by God, embedded in us so that our acts of love towards one another shines forth the very greatness of God.

> *"But whoso keepeth his word, in him verily is the love of God perfected: hereby know we that we are in him."* 1 John 2:5

From this godly union, we show in ourselves the faithfulness that God presents to us, and as scripture tells us, our love is perfected because we are in him. His faithfulness calls for us to remain in him, and if we remain in him, he is faithful and just to forgive us our sins. God, day in and day out, shines his mercy upon each of us, keeping us the all the days that he has numbered for us.

> *"Know therefore that the LORD thy God, he is God, the faithful God, which keepeth covenant and mercy with them that love him and keep his commandments to a thousand generations; And repayeth them that hate him to their face, to destroy them: he will not be slack to him that hateth him, he will repay him to his face."* Deuteronomy 7:9-10

From his word, we can read about his faithfulness, that he will always remain the same, for he does not change! God's faithfulness is the same today as it was yesterday and will be tomorrow.

> *"For I am the LORD, I change not; therefore ye sons of Jacob are not consumed."* Malachi 3:6

Man changes on a daily basis: his mind, his ways, his attitude, his faith, etc.; but lucky for us, God is not a man that he should lie:

> *"God is not a man, that he should lie; neither the son of man, that he should repent: hath he said, and shall he not do it? or hath he spoken, and shall he not make it good?"* Numbers 23:19

God is the same yesterday, today, and tomorrow. His love extends to us forever.

We learn from scripture that the Lord's faithfulness knows no limits and is there for all time. The Psalmist in Psalm 36:5 gives us a picture of this limitless faithfulness:

> *"Thy mercy, O LORD, is in the heavens; and thy faithfulness reacheth unto the clouds."*

"Thy faithfulness is unto all generations: thou hast established the earth, and it abideth." Psalm 119:90

Through God's faithfulness, we can see that his love is limitless and has no bounds. Can you say that you are that faithful and overflowing with exceeding love for mankind? God has said it, and he has proven it. Although we are born into sin, his everlasting love shines upon us in his mercy. We are undeserving of his faithfulness, but he gives it to us because of his love for us.

> *"It is of the LORD's mercies that we are not consumed, because his compassions fail not. They are new every morning: great is thy faithfulness. The LORD is my portion, saith my soul; therefore will I hope in him."* Lamentations 3:22-24

Paul tells us in Romans that none are righteous and that we are all worthy of judgment by the Father. But by God's grace, mercy, and love, he does not pour out his wrath upon us. The wording in Lamentations 3:22 is very strong—"consumed," which is to say that his wrath will overwhelm us and devour us like fire does paper. But because of his love, we have another chance to get right before him.

How can we repay the Lord for his faithfulness? How can we show him that we love him? By lending yourself to praise him with whatever you have to give:

> *"IT IS A GOOD THING TO GIVE THANKS UNTO THE LORD, AND TO SING PRAISES UNTO THY NAME, O MOST HIGH: To shew forth thy lovingkindness in the morning, and thy faithfulness every night, Upon an instrument of ten strings, and upon the psaltery; upon the harp with a solemn sound."* Psalm 92:1-3

REV. KELVIN MCKISIC

"But who so keepeth his word, in him verily is the love of God perfected: hereby know we that we are in him." 1 John 2:5

His Love Delivers

And the LORD said: "I have surely seen the oppression of My people who are in Egypt, and have heard their cry because of their taskmasters, for I know their sorrows. So I have come down to deliver them out of the hand of the Egyptians, and to bring them up from that land to a good and large land, to a land flowing with milk and honey, to the place of the Canaanites and the Hittites and the Amorites and the Perizzites and the Hivites and the Jebusites. Now therefore, behold, the cry of the children of Israel has come to Me, and I have also seen the oppression with which the Egyptians oppress them. Come now, therefore, and I will send you to Pharaoh that you may bring My people, the children of Israel, out of Egypt." Exodus 3:7-10

Moses was commissioned at the burning bush to be the agent of God to deliver the Hebrews from bondage from the Egyptians. First, we see the nature of God's love that claims us as his own when he says, "My people." This loving God looks down on his own, wanting the best for them, knowing that they had been through years of suffering.

Here we see that God not only wants to deliver his people from bondage, but to give them to a good and large land, a land of milk and honey. God's love for his people was shown to Moses in a supernatural way, via the burning bush, a sign that this was indeed God, a sign that something wonderful and loving was to take place.

Now Moses was tending the flock of Jethro his father-in-law, the priest of Midian. And he led the flock to the back of the desert, and came to Horeb, the mountain of God. And the Angel of the LORD appeared to him in a flame of fire from the midst of a bush. So he looked, and behold, the bush was burning with fire, but the bush was not consumed. Then Moses said, "I will now turn aside and see this great sight, why the bush does not burn." So when the LORD saw that he turned aside to look, God called to him from the midst of the bush and said, "Moses, Moses!" And he said, "Here I am." Exodus 3:1-4

If we look closely at the story of Moses, we will find that he was also delivered from bondage, a bondage of guilt and shame for his murdering an Egyptian. God's love allowed the years to pass, giving Moses time to learn how to lead.

I AM YOURS AND YOU ARE MINE: GOD'S LOVE

"Come now, therefore, and I will send you to Pharaoh that you may bring My people, the children of Israel, out of Egypt." Exodus 3:10

God's love led Moses to the land of Midian, where Moses would become son-in-law to the priest of Midian and learn to be a shepherd of the people by first learning to be a shepherd of sheep. Because of God's love for each of us, he will always prepare a way for you, just as he did for Moses. His love will not send you into the world without first giving you the tools needed to complete the task he has for you. In his love, we are delivered from this world, just as the children of Israel and Moses were delivered from the Egyptians.

As you read more in the book of Exodus, you find that God gave Moses help to overcome his mental, emotional, and physical disadvantages. First, we see that Moses asks God why Pharaoh would listen to him.

> *But Moses said to God, "Who am I that I should go to Pharaoh, and that I should bring the children of Israel out of Egypt?" Exodus 3:11*

God then tells Moses that it does not matter who he is; God will be with him, and Moses would be a sign that he is a messenger from God. God's love does not leave you alone to fight the battle or complete the task; he is with you always. Moses tells the Lord that he is not a good speaker and is unable to deliver the words that God wants him to say.

> *"Then Moses said to the LORD, "O my Lord, I am not eloquent, neither before nor since You have spoken to Your servant; but I am slow of speech and slow of tongue." Exodus 4:11*

But again, our God is loving and caring, letting Moses know that God has everything under control, that God is the creator of man and can give to Moses what he needs to accomplish the task. And as we read in the book of Exodus, we find that God is indeed faithful, and the children of Israel do reach the Promised Land. We should look back on our lives and see how God has delivered us. Look back and see how he helped us through our worst troubles and delivered us, just as he did for the children of Israel. In his love, we are delivered.

> *"Giving thanks unto the Father, which hath made us meet to be partakers of the inheritance of the saints in light: Who hath delivered us from the power of darkness, and hath translated us into the kingdom of his dear Son: In whom we have redemption through his blood, even the forgiveness of sins: Who is the image of the invisible God, the firstborn of every creature: For by him were all things created, that are in heaven, and that are in earth, visible and invisible, whether they be thrones, or dominions, or principalities, or powers: all things were created by him, and for him: And he is before all things, and by him all things consist." Colossians 1:12-17*

Because of God's great love, we are given an inheritance in his kingdom, being counted as his children, brothers of Christ. It is because Christ cares for us that we have been ransomed from the hands of the evil one and brought back under the care of our loving and merciful Father in Heaven. And it is because of his love that we exist.

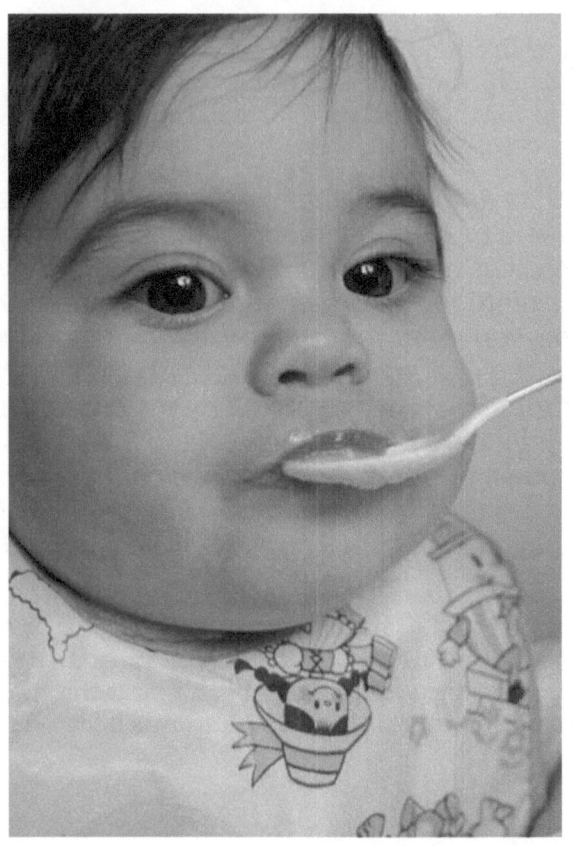

"God having provided some better thing for us, that they without us should not be made perfect." Hebrews 11:40

His Love Provides

The children of Israel wandered through the dessert for forty years, in what started out as an eleven-day walk to the Promised Land. God did not force them to wander for forty years, but their stiff-necked ways and hardened hearts kept them from reaching the land promised to them.

We read in the book of Exodus how God provided for the children as they wandered through the wilderness on their way to the Promised Land. God's first provision was when the Egyptians gave the Israelites great wealth before they left Egypt.

> *"And I will give this people favour in the sight of the Egyptians: and it shall come to pass, that, when ye go, ye shall not go empty. But every woman shall borrow of her neighbour, and of her that sojourneth in her house, jewels of silver, and jewels of gold, and raiment: and ye shall put them upon your sons, and upon your daughters; and ye shall spoil the Egyptians." Exodus 3:21-22*

God, in his infinite love, had already provided for the children of Israel before they set forth on their journey. When they left Egypt, they left with many riches and herds.

God provided for the Israelites a pillar of fire by night and a cloud by day as they traveled to the Red Sea. His provisions gave them light in the darkest night and shade in the heat of day. His love has also shined in the darkness of your life to provide you a way out without stumbling. His love has shielded you from the evil one, giving you relief from the sting of death.

Once the Israelites made it across the Red Sea, God gave them water. The source was bitter, or poisonous, but God in his love told Moses to take a branch from a tree to sweeten or cleanse the water so that they had fresh water to drink. God provided for them, keeping them alive during the harsh journey to the Promised Land:

- He told Moses to strike a rock to bring forth water for them to drink
- He rained down bread from Heaven each day
- He cause quail to rest upon the ground so they could have meat
- He kept their clothing and shoes from wearing out
- He gave them a snake on a pole to gaze upon when they were bitten so that they would get well.
- He provided for their victory in the many battles along their way

God has done the same thing for you in your life; look where you come from and at the things that you have. He has given us many provisions for our journey.

> *"And Abraham said, My son, God will provide himself a lamb for a burnt offering: so they went both of them together." Genesis 22:8*

For our sins, God's love provided us a way, another ram in the bush, Christ Jesus. Christ Jesus laid his life on the line for us because he loved us. And Jesus came to earth because God so loved us. In his love, we are given provisions for an eternal life, a life where we will once again walk in the glory of the Father.

It is said, "God always has another ram in the bush." In Genesis 22, Abraham is told by God to sacrifice his son Isaac. In verse 7, we see Abraham's words after Isaac asks where the lamb that will be sacrificed is. In this story, when Abraham was ready to sacrifice his beloved son, God provided a ram at the last moment. God's love indeed provides, giving us his mercy and grace so that we can sacrifice ourselves for his pleasure. Because of his love, we are to live our lives as holy sacrifices, pleasing before our loving Father in heaven.

In 1 Kings 17, we read of the story of a widow gathering sticks so that she could prepare a last meal. But the Lord planned to show his love through the provisions that he would supply the widow. In this story, God sent Elijah to her in her time of need. In all his ways, God is forever providing for his children. The widow's barrel of wheat never went empty, and the oil never went low; this God did to provide for the widow and her child. Out of his infinite love, God gives in abundance to those that fear him.

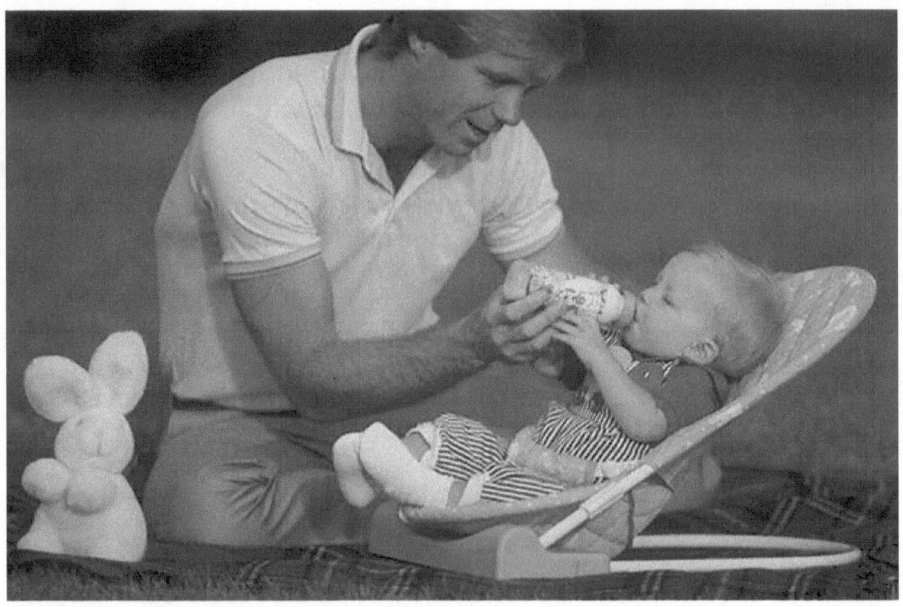

"But whoso hath this world's good, and seeth his brother have need, and shutteth up his bowels of compassion from him, how dwelleth the love of God in him? My little children, let us not love in word, neither in tongue; but in deed and in truth." 1 John 3:17-18

The book of Matthew also contains two wonderful stories of God's love in provision. In this gospel, we read how Jesus in his compassion feeds a group of four thousand men and another of five thousand. Here again, we see Jesus' love for those who had not eaten, and from a few fish and some loaves of bread, he fed a multitude. With God, nothing is impossible and in our times of need, he is there to give us the things we need for our day and our life.

I AM YOURS AND YOU ARE MINE: GOD'S LOVE

"But my God shall supply all your need according to his riches in glory by Christ Jesus." Philippians 4:19

In His Love Are Planned Provisions

Let us look at how much God loves us. Look in the book of Genesis, starting at the 37th chapter. Here a story unfolds of God's love and how it put Joseph in the hands of the Egyptians, so that when a severe famine came, Joseph was in a position to help his family. As we read the account of Joseph, we find that his brothers sell him to slave traders, who in turn sell him to Potiphar, an Egyptian officer of Pharaoh's, a captain of the guard. Joseph worked for Potiphar until he was thrown into prison; Potiphar's wife wanted to have sexual relations with Joseph, but Joseph refused, and in her scorn brought charges of rape against Joseph. Until this incident, Potiphar was fond of Joseph and had him run all of his affairs. While in prison, Joseph runs the prison. God's love still shines, even though things look terrible for Joseph, but these seemingly terrible things are God's way of training Joseph for the final roll that he will play in God's plan. Later, Pharaoh lets Joseph out of prison because Joseph interpreted one of his dreams. Joseph tells Pharaoh that the dreams relate to a famine that will hit Egypt for seven years and that he should spend this time to store provisions.

Not only does God plan for our material provisions, He also plans for our very existence. We can see this plan in the book of Esther, where evil plans are underway to destroy the nation of Jews. But God's love had a plan in the works to keep His people safe.

The story of God's provision begins with the exile of the Israelite people in chapters 24 & 25 of 2 Kings, and His planned provision of deliverance from extinction is given in the book of Esther.

While the Jews are being held captive in Babylon, the area is conquered by the Medes and the Persians. Under the Persian king Cyrus, the Jews are given the opportunity to return to Jerusalem.

Please note God's plan, as King Cyrus is spoken of by God to be His instrument some 70 years before the Jews are set free.

> *"That saith of Cyrus, He is my shepherd, and shall perform all my pleasure: even saying to Jerusalem, Thou shalt be built; and to the temple, Thy foundation shall be laid." Isaiah 44:28*

But only a small amount of the Israelite population takes advantage of the offer to return. Ezra and Nehemiah give accounts of those who do return, but most choose the prosperity and luxury of Persia, and remain behind. Dr. J. Vernon McGee states that "While these Jews are out of the will of God, they are not beyond the care of God, and so the book of Esther is about the providence of God." It is by way of God's love that He provides the means for a Jewish woman, Esther, to become the Queen of Persia. Now, there is a person named Haman who was given great power by the King Ahasuerus. While in this position of power Haman devises a way to destroy the Israelite population. Haman then basically tricks the king into putting the plan into motion. But because of God's provision of making Esther queen the plan is brought down and Haman was hanged for his evil doings.

The plan of provision extends to Esther as she appears before the king without an appointment.

> *Go, gather together all the Jews that are present in Shushan, and fast ye for me, and neither eat nor drink three days, night or day: I also and my maidens will fast likewise; and so will I go in unto the king, which is not according to the law: and if I perish, I perish. Esther 4:16*

REV. KELVIN MCKISIC

But thou, O Lord, art a God full of compassion, and gracious, long suffering, and plenteous in mercy and truth. Psalm 86:15

His Longsuffering Love

> *But you, O LORD, are a compassionate and gracious God, slow to anger, abounding in love and faithfulness.* Psalm 86:15

Throughout the scriptures, God's love is patient and forgiving. As we read the stories of the children of Israel wandering through the desert, we see God being patient through their complaints and grumblings. He provides for their needs by giving them food to eat and clothes that never wear out.

God, through his love for us, has given us mercy and grace: mercy in not giving us the punishment we deserve, grace in giving us the things we don't deserve. *"he does not treat us as our sin deserve or repay us according to our iniquities."* Psalm 103:10

In the book of Matthew, Peter asks Jesus, "Lord, how many times shall I forgive my brother when he sins against me? Up to seven times?" Jesus replies, "I tell you, not seven times, but seventy-seven times." In Matthew 18:21-35, we find the longsuffering love of God. As we look upon our own lives, we see that God's love has forgiven us many times over for things for which we rightly should be punished. We need to start taking stock in his love and live the life he has called us to live.

> *Yet the LORD longs to be gracious to you; he rises to show you compassion. For the LORD is a God of justice. Blessed are all who wait for him!* Isaiah 30:18

In his suffering he allows us, through his permissive will, to go our own way, to bump our heads into the wall, to stumble and fall; this is done to show us how much we need him in our lives. This he does with great love for us, knowing that in the end we will come to our senses and turn back to him who loves us. In the book of Luke Jesus shares a parable that gives us a picture of how God waits for us to return to him, how his love and compassion saves us from the judgment our sin-ridden lives deserve.

> *Then he told them this parable: "A man had a fig tree, planted in his vineyard, and he went to look for fruit on it, but did not find any. So he said to the man who took care of the vineyard, 'For three years now I've been coming to look for fruit on this fig tree and haven't found any. Cut it down! Why should it use up the soil?' 'Sir,' the man replied, 'leave it alone for one more year, and I'll dig around it and fertilize it. If it bears fruit next year, fine! If not, then cut it down." Luke 13:6-9*

Because God loves us, he allows us time to get ourselves right with him. And as the parable goes, we are also given a helper, someone to tend to us and care for us, to fertilize us as we bear the good fruits that God looks for.

> *The LORD is not slow in keeping his promise, as some understand slowness. He is patient with you, not wanting anyone to perish, but everyone to come to repentance. 2 Peter 3:9*

God will call his children home one day. Christ Jesus will one day rapture us to meet him in the clouds, at which time we will be changed in the twinkling of an eye to be like him. The Father's suffering will end. This time marks the beginning of the period of tribulation, in which God will rain down wrath upon those who willing rebelled against his grace, those who have aligned themselves with the evil one. But because of his love, God will still gives those left behind a chance to repent and accept his love, to be dressed in white robes. Have you accepted his gift of salvation? Is your name written in the book of life? Will you be caught up in the clouds with

Christ Jesus? If your answer to these questions is no, then right now pray this prayer:

Father, forgive my sins.
Jesus, come into my heart.
Make me the kind of person you want me to be.
Thank you for saving me.

Now if you prayed and meant it sincerely, you are now a child of God. It's that simple! God loves you so that all you need to do is admit you're a sinner and ask him for forgiveness.

**Father, forgive my sins.
Jesus, come into my heart.
Make me the kind of person you want me to be.
Thank you for saving me.**

His Love Forgives

> *"The LORD saw how great man's wickedness on the earth had become, and that every inclination of the thoughts of his heart was only evil all the time." Genesis 6:5*

God grieved and felt sorry that he had created man. No one can grieve unless he or she first loved. God's heart was broken by mankind's evil desires; God's love was trampled upon by mankind's continued disobedience.

The Lord wanted to destroy all life, both man and animal. But God looked upon the earth and saw Noah, in whom God found grace. He did not want to see this righteous man die. God's love spared the lives of Noah and his family because Noah was just and perfect in his generation.

> *"How priceless is your unfailing love! Both high and low among men find refuge in the shadow of your wings." Psalm 36:7*

Noah put his trust in God and built the ark as God commanded. The love of God saved mankind so that we can know how much he does love us. How can God show his love for us if we are not around to see it?

God loves us in spite of ourselves. He gives us his grace and his mercy; he knows that we will fall short of his glory, and his love provides for that. His love never fails, and it covers a multitude of sins. God's love is a forgiving love; he forgives us our sins when we come to him in prayer and forgets it once we have repented with a true heart.

> *"Blessed is he whose transgressions are forgiven, whose sins are covered. Blessed is the man whose sin the Lord does not count against him and in whose spirit is no deceit." Psalm 32:2-3*

I AM YOURS AND YOU ARE MINE: GOD'S LOVE

"The LORD is compassionate and gracious, slow to anger, abounding in love. He will not always accuse, nor harbor his anger forever; he does not treat us as our sins deserve or repay us according to our iniquities. For as high as the heavens are above the earth, so great is his love for those who fear him; as far as the east is from the west, so far has he removed our transgressions from us." Psalm 103:8-12

We are a rebellious people, bent on doing the things that appeal to us. We continually fight against the will of God to follow our hearts' desires. But through it all, God shows his love for us by giving us chance after chance to do what is right in his eyes. His love is long-suffering, wanting all of mankind to be saved, wishing that none of us should perish.

His Love Flows with Compassion and Grace

"Rend your heart and not your garments. Return to God, for he is gracious and compassionate, slow to anger and abounding in love, and he relents from sending calamity." Joel 2:13

We have all fallen short of the glory of God, but his love for us keeps us. He fixes the broken parts of our lives and strengthens us for the next hurdle. How many times have you thought that God could not love someone like you? Knowing the things that you have done? Well, God does love you, and if you ask him with a sincere heart, he will forgive your sins and make you whole again. Look at King David, the bloodline of Jesus. David was a murder and adulterer. But he opened his heart in prayer and thanksgiving to God, and God blessed David, giving him the promise of the Messiah being of his seed. So no matter what troubles and problems you may have had in your life, God is there, waiting to wipe the tears from your eyes and make all things new for you. Turn to God and feel the cleansing of his love upon your life.

"Rend your heart and not your garments. Return to God, for he is gracious and compassionate, slow to anger and abounding in love, and he relents from sending calamity." Joel 2:13

In His Love We Are Cared For

God in his infinite love has provided everything that we could possible need in life and beyond. The book of Revelation tells us we will live in a beautiful city with God.

Adam, in the garden, experienced this when he walked with God in the cool of the evening. We should long to do the same, Father and child, walking together, talking of things that bring them joy. God longs to walk again with us in the cool of the evening; this we know because of all of the work he does to free us from the grips of sin, the one thing that separates us from God. He loves us and wants to gather us to him again.

God wants us to ask for the desires of our heart; he will grant it. Give your heart to him and praise him; he cares for you and wants you to be free.

> "Praise the LORD, O my soul; all my inmost being, praise his holy name. Praise the LORD, O my soul and forget not all his benefits – who forgives all your sins and heals all your diseases, who redeems your life from the pit and crowns you with love and compassion, who satisfies your desires with good things so that your youth is renewed like the eagle's."
> Psalm 103:1-5

We see the depths of God's love for us by looking at the things done for the children of Israel as they wandered in the wilderness.

- They cried for water; God turned bitter water sweet so that they could drink. Exodus 15:22-25
- They were hungry, and he feed them with manna and quail. Exodus 16:4-15
- God provided water from rocks. Exodus 17:5-6

- God helps them defeat their enemies
- Moses is allowed to see the Promised Land
- God leads them into the Promised Land

For some of us, our lives seem like we are wandering in the wilderness, looking for our Promised Land. But fear not; God loves you and knows you. He knew you before you were conceived, and he knows the number of hairs on your head.

He knows your thoughts: God knows you better than you know yourself, and he wants you to come to him with everything in prayer. He knows that we battle the physical world, but he wants us to overcome it. *"The LORD knows the thoughts of man; he knows that they are futile."* **Psalm 94:11** God, knowing our frailty, wants to help us help ourselves. He knows our thoughts are limited, but his thoughts for us are limitless.

He knows your fears: *"I sought the LORD, and he answered me; he delivered me from all my fears."* **Psalm 34:4** God knows your fears and troubles and is waiting for you to turn to him for comfort. He will wipe the tears from your eyes and turn back the thing that brings you fear. God does not want you to live in fear of anything; and by living in his love, we are given freedom from fear.

He knows your desires: God wants to give you abundance—a life that allows you to want for nothing. The desires of your heart will be granted if you seek him with all your heart and desire things that are good and pleasing to him. God in his love will sometimes keep the thing we desire from us because he knows that it may not be good for us. Be thankful to God that he has answered your desires. He will answer you with a yes, no, or not right now. He always acts in our best interest. That is the characteristic of a loving Father; he will give you only the desires that will not cause you harm. *"For your Father knows what you need before you ask him."* **Matthew 6:8b**

He will provide for you, if you trust him wholeheartedly: God wants to care and provide for you, giving you all the things you need for your day. Remember how God provided for the children of Israel by giving them manna every day? And how the manna would only last a day; any left for the next day was rotten. This is how God shows us that he will provide for us every day. In Matthew 6:9-13 we are given the way to pray. Verse 11 asks God to give us our daily bread. This bread is more than then a physical meal to be taken by mouth. It is also a spiritual meal for our souls.

> "Our Father in heaven, hallowed by your name, your kingdom come, your will be done on earth as it is in heaven. Give us today our daily bread. Forgive us our debts, as we also forgive our debtors. And lead us not into temptation, but deliver us from the evil one." Matthew 6:9-13

He will protect you, if you trust him with all your heart: "The LORD will keep you from all harm – he will watch over your life; the LORD will watch over your coming and going both now and forevermore." Psalm 121:7-8 God wants to secure your path and protect you from any hurt, harm, or danger. His love is that great for his children. What loving father wants to see their children hurt? Why would our Father in heaven act any different?

> "The LORD is a refuge for the oppressed, a stronghold in times of trouble. Those who know your name will trust in you, for you, LORD, have never forsaken those who seek you." Psalm 9:9-10

God wants to take you in his arms and give you the loving care you want and need. Turn to him and open your heart.

"For God so loved the world that he gave his one and only Son, that whoever believes in him shall not perish but have eternal life." John 3:16

His Love Brought Us Jesus

"For God so loved the world that he gave his one and only Son, that whoever believes in him shall not perish but have eternal life." John 3:16

Through Adam came sin, and death through sin. Through Jesus came life. The death through sin is more than physical death, in which the soul separates from the physical body. Death from sin is an eternal death, in which you are separated from God. Jesus brings an eternal life, in which our soul lives with and worships the Father, a life of joy, a life where sickness does not exist, where pain is unheard of, where we all live in peace and happiness. This eternal life is given through God's love for us.

God's love sent us Jesus to bear the burden of our sins, to die on the cross as the last perfect sacrifice, to bear the pain, suffering, and humiliation, so that we could have eternal life.

I AM YOURS AND YOU ARE MINE: GOD'S LOVE

"For he shall grow up before him as a tender plant, and as a root out of a dry ground: he hath no form nor comeliness; and when we shall see him, there is no beauty that we should desire him."
Isaiah 53:2

His Love Gives Us an Example to Live By

> *"Let this mind be in you, which was also in Christ Jesus: Who, being in the form of God, thought it not robbery to be equal with God: But made himself of no reputation, and took upon him the form of a servant, and was made in the likeness of men: And being found in fashion as a man, he humbled himself, and became obedient unto death, even the death of the cross." Philippians 2:5-8*

God in his love for us did not leave us without an example to follow in our reconciliation with him. God gave us Christ Jesus as a savior, as well as an example for us to follow. In Paul's letter to the Philippians, he tells them to have the mind of Christ Jesus, who left his throne in heaven to become a servant of mankind. As Paul writes, we should look to the way Christ lived and the things he did so that we can follow his example in how he treated others.

> *"As obedient children, not fashioning yourselves according to the former lusts in your ignorance: But as he which hath called you is holy, so be ye holy in all manner of conversation; Because it is written, Be ye holy; for I am holy." 1 Peter 1:15*

God's love gave us the model of life so that we can return to the way he created us, in his image. His love desires us to be again as he created us: "Be ye holy; for I am holy." We were created in his love so that we could also show love. Christ came to love, heal, and forgive, which he does because of his love for the world as well as to set the model for us to live.

Let us not walk in the life that we did before we came to the saving knowledge of Christ. Let us get back to the way that God created us. Let us see the image in which God created us through Christ Jesus, who was God in the flesh. God in his great love for us stepped down from eternity into time so that we could once again walk in the cool of the evening with him.

"As obedient children, not fashioning yourselves according to the former lusts in your ignorance: But as he which hath called you is holy, so be ye holy in all manner of conversation; Because it is written, Be ye holy; for I am holy." 1 Peter 1:15

Healings Come from His Love

"And, behold, there was a woman which had a spirit of infirmity eighteen years, and was bowed together, and could in no wise lift up herself. And when Jesus saw her, he called her to him, and said unto her, Woman, thou art loosed from thine infirmity. And he laid his hands on her: and immediately she was made straight, and glorified God." Luke 13:11-13

Here we see the wonders of God's love for his people. In this story, a woman was bent over and could not walk upright for eighteen years. And from the scriptures, it does not look as though she was seeking Jesus for help, but our Lord saw her and called upon her and healed her. This show of our Lord's love did not require her to do a thing but come to him when he called her.

Like the woman in the story, we are all bent over. Since sin took hold of us, it has caused us to not be in the shape that God originally started us. But there is hope for an uplifted state. It is by way of his love, a love that wants us to be healed from all of our sicknesses and problems. All that is required is that you come to him when he calls you. His love does not demand that you do what man asks of you; all his love calls for is for us to come when he calls. God's love sent Jesus Christ to teach, heal, and forgive us. Through his love, we find a healing to the physical, spiritual, emotional, social, and financial areas of our lives—all because he loved us before we loved him.

REV. KELVIN MCKISIC

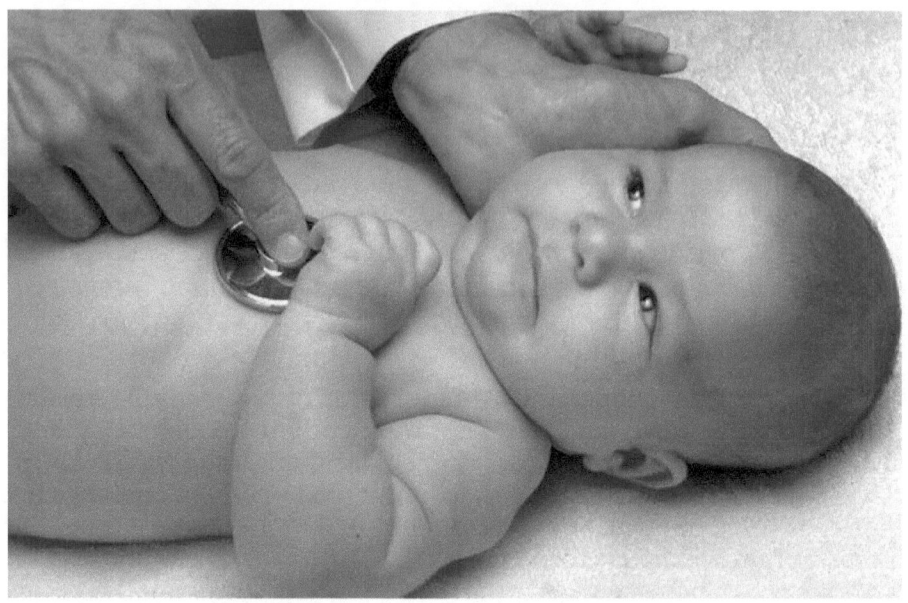

"And, behold, there was a woman which had a spirit of infirmity eighteen years, and was bowed together, and could in no wise lift up herself. And when Jesus saw her, he called her to him, and said unto her, Woman, thou art loosed from thine infirmity. And he laid his hands on her: and immediately she was made straight, and glorified God." Luke 13:11-13

By His Love Our Faith Brings Healing

"And it came to pass, that as he was come nigh unto Jericho, a certain blind man sat by the way side begging: And hearing the multitude pass by, he asked what it meant. And they told him, that Jesus of Nazareth passeth by. And he cried, saying, Jesus, thou son of David, have mercy on me. And they which went before rebuked him, that he should hold his peace: but he cried so much the more, Thou son of David, have mercy on me. And Jesus stood, and commanded him to be brought unto him: and when he was come near, he asked him, Saying, What wilt thou that I shall do unto thee? And he said, Lord, that I may receive my sight. And Jesus said unto him, Receive thy sight: thy faith hath saved thee. And immediately he received his sight, and followed him, glorifying God: and all the people, when they saw it, gave praise unto God." Luke 18:35-43

Jesus tells the man that by his faith he is saved. Why did Jesus not say, "Thy faith hath healed thee?" Because God's love does not stop at healing the physical condition, it goes deeper. The blind man's faith, as with all of our faith, is the foundation on which our healings rest—faith in Christ Jesus. The blind man's faith was there before Jesus came to the city of Jericho, as the blind man was told that the reason for all the commotion was that Jesus of Nazareth was passing by. For the blind man, Jesus of Nazareth meant much more to him than just some person from a town; the blind man knew Jesus as the prophesied Son of God because he says, "Thou son of David." Here again is God's love allowed to work on us by believing that Jesus is who he says he is and believing that he can do what God can do. The blind man believed this, and his faith was there long before Jesus came to Jericho.

God healings bring about complete healing. We do not know what happened to the man after he received his sight, but we know that his emotional and spiritual states were no longer the same, because he glorified God and gave much praise. He at one time sat in the dark, both physical darkness and emotional darkness, but is now able to see light, and with that light he has a new outlook on life. He is able to work like any other person in his city, to move about just as freely. He is free from the bondage of blindness because Jesus, the light of the world, shined upon him.

> *"Then spake Jesus again unto them, saying, I am the light of the world: he that followeth me shall not walk in darkness, but shall have the light of life." John 8:12*

In Christ Jesus, we find the embodiment of God's love. And in that love, we see that our Father in Heaven does not want us to live life in a dark and hopeless state. Because he loves us, he wants our lives to be better. In his love, we can find healing from our sin-ridden state. In his love, we can be made whole again.

> *"And, behold, a woman, which was diseased with an issue of blood twelve years, came behind him, and touched the hem of his garment: For she said within herself, If I may but touch his garment, I shall be whole. But Jesus turned him about, and when he saw her, he said, Daughter, be of good comfort; thy faith hath made thee whole. And the woman was made whole from that hour." Matthew 9:20-22*

I AM YOURS AND YOU ARE MINE: GOD'S LOVE

Again, we see that by our faith in Jesus Christ, we find healing, all because God loved us before we loved him. This woman's twelve years of suffering ended once she believed in God. In this, we see a complete healing: physical, mental, emotional, and spiritual. In the culture of this woman's day, she was not allowed to be amongst the people because her condition rendered her unclean. So for those twelve years, she suffered from the physical problem, a low emotional state, and from a low spiritual state. Then she heard about Jesus of Nazareth, and upon hearing about him, her faith brought her out into the public, where she could have been stoned for her uncleanness; faith in Jesus Christ allowed her to know that he could heal her. By the hem of his garment, she was made complete. By God's love for us, she was given a new lease on life, new hope for tomorrow. She was a new creature, saved by the love of God.

By His Word We Are Healed

> *"Then they cry unto the LORD in their trouble, and he saveth them out of their distresses. He sent his word, and healed them, and delivered them from their destructions." Psalm 107:19-20*

By his loving word alone can we find relief from the distresses and troubles of our lives. God loves us so much that he does not require us to do anything but ask of him and believe that it will be done, and in his love, he delivers us.

> *"And when Jesus was entered into Capernaum, there came unto him a centurion, beseeching him, 6And saying, Lord, my servant lieth at home sick of the palsy, grievously tormented. And Jesus saith unto him, I will come and heal him. The centurion answered and said, Lord, I am not worthy that thou shouldest come under my roof: but speak the word only, and my servant shall be healed. For I am a man under authority, having soldiers under me: and I say to this man, Go, and he goeth; and to another, Come, and he cometh; and to my servant, Do this, and he doeth it. When Jesus heard it, he marvelled, and said to them that followed, Verily I say unto you, I have not found so great faith, no, not in Israel. And I say unto you, That many shall come from the east and west, and shall sit down with Abraham, and Isaac, and Jacob, in the kingdom of heaven. But the children of the kingdom shall be cast out into outer darkness: there shall be weeping and gnashing of teeth. And Jesus said unto the centurion, Go thy way; and as thou hast believed, so be it done unto thee. And his servant was healed in the selfsame hour." Matthew 8:8-13*

By the word of Jesus, the servant was healed. The gentile centurion believed that Jesus could heal without ever seeing or touching the person. The centurion knew that all he had to do was ask, because he was aware that the love that flowed from Jesus did not care about ethnicity or skin color. The love of Jesus was for all people, righteous or sinner.

His Love Is Inseparable

"Who shall separate us from the love of Christ? shall tribulation, or distress, or persecution, or famine, or nakedness, or peril, or sword? As it is written, For thy sake we are killed all the day long; we are accounted as sheep for the slaughter." Romans 8:35-36

Sin desired to kill us, but the love of Christ keeps us safe. His love is so great that nothing can separate us from it. In his love, we find shelter from the harms of the world. In his love, we find rest from troubles. Who or what can separate us from his mighty love? Although we go through each day with the evil one trying to take us out, we have Christ as our protector, guardian, and guide, all because he loved us first.

I AM YOURS AND YOU ARE MINE: GOD'S LOVE

"Who shall separate us from the love of Christ? shall tribulation, or distress, or persecution, or famine, or nakedness, or peril, or sword? As it is written, For thy sake we are killed all the day long; we are accounted as sheep for the slaughter." Romans 8:35-36

His Love Does Not Forget

"But Zion said, The LORD hath forsaken me, and my Lord hath forgotten me. Can a woman forget her sucking child, that she should not have compassion on the son of her womb? yea, they may forget, yet will I not forget thee. Behold, I have graven thee upon the palms of my hands; thy walls are continually before me." Isaiah 49:14-16

We cry out to the Lord in our time of despair, feeling that he has forgotten or forsaken us. But no, his love keeps us close to his bosom and rescues us in our time of need. Isaiah 49:14-16 paints a beautiful picture of how God will no more forget us than a mother would forget to care for her infant child.

God's love is so wonderful that he has engraved you upon the palms of his hands, your life continually watched by him. As a mother watches over her young, so God watches over us. His love never leaves and never forsakes.

"All that the Father giveth me shall come to me; and him that cometh to me I will in no wise cast out." John 6:37

Because of his love for us, Jesus will never cast us aside.

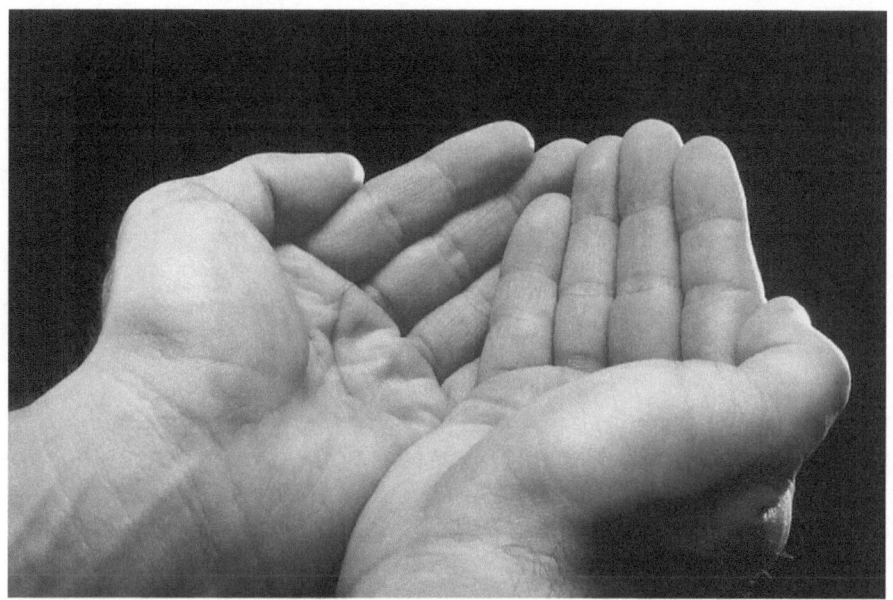

"But Zion said, The LORD hath forsaken me, and my Lord hath forgotten me. Can a woman forget her sucking child, that she should not have compassion on the son of her womb? yea, they may forget, yet will I not forget thee. Behold, I have graven thee upon the palms of my hands; thy walls are continually before me." Isaiah 49:14-16

He Loved Us First

> "Herein is love, not that we loved God, but that he loved us, and sent his Son to be the propitiation for our sins." 1 John 4:10

The apostle John makes it very clear what the essence of love is. God loved us before we loved him; even if we never come to love him, he still loves us.

> "And it came to pass, as Jesus sat at meat in the house, behold, many publicans and sinners came and sat down with him and his disciples. And when the Pharisees saw it, they said unto his disciples, Why eateth your Master with publicans and sinners? But when Jesus heard that, he said unto them, They that be whole need not a physician, but they that are sick." Matthew 9:10-12

His love wants to heal us of our sinfulness. He came to heal, love, and forgive. He came to die to buy our pardon because he loved us.

We deserved punishment for our carnal ways, but Jesus died for us, the ransom for our sins. This is what God had planned in the Garden of Eden—for Christ to come to earth so that we could be saved. There is no greater love than this. God loved us first!

"And it came to pass, as Jesus sat at meat in the house, behold, many publicans and sinners came and sat down with him and his disciples. And when the Pharisees saw it, they said unto his disciples, Why eateth your Master with publicans and sinners? But when Jesus heard that, he said unto them, They that be whole need not a physician, but they that are sick." Matthew 9:10-12

A Self-sacrificing Love

"Greater love has no one than this, that he lay down his life for his friends. You are my friends if you do what I command." John 15:13-14

What greater show of one's love is there than to die to save a friend's life? Jesus showed this kind of love for us by willingly going to the cross to save us from the wrath of God. For must of us, it is hard to loan money, let alone die for them. But Jesus shows us that his is the greater love; he would shed his blood so that we could be free from the bondage of sin.

"I am crucified with Christ: nevertheless I live; yet not I, but Christ liveth in me: and the life which I now live in the flesh I live by the faith of the Son of God, who loved me, and gave himself for me." Galatians 2:20

We have a life free from the ownership of sin because Christ sacrificed himself for us. We are renewed every day, thanks to his love for us, that we should not perish, but have everlasting life.

"I am crucified with Christ: nevertheless I live; yet not I, but Christ liveth in me: and the life which I now live in the flesh I live by the faith of the Son of God, who loved me, and gave himself for me." Galatians 2:20

An Everlasting Love

"Now before the feast of the passover, when Jesus knew that his hour was come that he should depart out of this world unto the Father, having loved his own which were in the world, he loved them unto the end." John 13:1

How many people do you know that would willingly die for you, and love you all the way to their death? Christ Jesus is the one! He was sent to us by God because he so loved us. With Jesus, there is no end; he is eternal, which means that he still loves us while sitting at the right-hand of the Father. He is eternal and loves us unto the end, which means that his love is there for us, saving us from the accusations of the evil one, an advocate for us to the Father.

His love is forever, never fading, regardless if our love fades for him. His love remains unchanging.

I AM YOURS AND YOU ARE MINE: GOD'S LOVE

"Now before the feast of the passover, when Jesus knew that his hour was come that he should depart out of this world unto the Father, having loved his own which were in the world, he loved them unto the end." John 13:1

"For God sent not his Son into the world to condemn the world; but that the world through him might be saved." John 3:17

We Are Saved by His Love

"For God sent not his Son into the world to condemn the world; but that the world through him might be saved." John 3:17

Jesus did not come to judge or destroy the world, but to save it and bring it back to the Father. Is that not showing great love for you? The Father, who was wronged by our disobedience and has every right to destroy us all, has decided that he will forgive us and provide a way for us to be reconciled to him. Christ Jesus is the means by which we are to be saved, and please note that the Bible speaks of the whole world—not just certain people, but all people.

And it shall come to pass, that whosoever shall call on the name of the Lord shall be saved. Acts 2:21

Neither is there salvation in any other: for there is none other name under heaven given among men, whereby we must be saved. Acts 4:12

Our hope for an eternal life is laid out just that simply. Believe in Jesus Christ. Believe that he died for our sins and rose again from the dead. Because God loves us so, he sent his son Jesus to pardon us of our sins. And it is only because God loves us so.

Take hold of the love that God has for us; it is free to all that call upon the name of Jesus. Call upon his name today so that you, too, can be saved.

The Bible is Love

Love is the most written about, sung about, agonized over, cherished, and philosophical subject in the entire world. Man has, down through the ages, misunderstood the nature of love, and in so doing have lost sight of the love that God has for us and wants us to project. The Bible has much to say about love because it is the Word of God, who is love.

God is love and by the Holy Spirit, he makes his love reside in us.

"He that loveth not knoweth not God; for God is love." 1 John 4:8

"And hope maketh not ashamed; because the love of God is shed abroad in our hearts by the Holy Ghost which is given unto us." Romans 5:5

God so loved the world that he sent his only son so that we might not perish but have eternal life.

"For God so loved the world, that he gave his only begotten Son, that whosoever believeth in him sho`uld not perish, but have everlasting life." John 3:16

"And hope maketh not ashamed; because the love of God is shed abroad in our hearts by the Holy Ghost which is given unto us." Romans 5:5

Love Is the Highest

Love is meant to be the highest human experience, greater than faith and hope. A true love is kind, it endures through all situations; it always hopes, it always believes, it is long-suffering, and it always rejoices in the truth.

> *"Though I speak with the tongues of men and of angels, and have not charity, I am become as sounding brass, or a tinkling cymbal. And though I have the gift of prophecy, and understand all mysteries, and all knowledge; and though I have all faith, so that I could remove mountains, and have not charity, I am nothing. And though I bestow all my goods to feed the poor, and though I give my body to be burned, and have not charity, it profiteth me nothing. Charity suffereth long, and is kind; charity envieth not; charity vaunteth not itself, is not puffed up, Doth not behave itself unseemly, seeketh not her own, is not easily provoked, thinketh no evil; Rejoiceth not in iniquity, but rejoiceth in the truth; Beareth all things, believeth all things, hopeth all things, endureth all things. Charity never faileth: but whether there be prophecies, they shall fail; whether there be tongues, they shall cease; whether there be knowledge, it shall vanish away. For we know in part, and we prophesy in part. But when that which is perfect is come, then that which is in part shall be done away. When I was a child, I spake as a child, I understood as a child, I thought as a child: but when I became a man, I put away childish things. For now we see through a glass, darkly; but then face to face: now I know in part; but then shall I know even as also I am known. And now abideth faith, hope, charity, these three; but the greatest of these is charity." 1 Corinthians 13*

God's Love Is a Perfect Love

A perfect love lies in the knowledge of God and in God, there is no fear; it is the covering for a multitude of sins.

> *"Beloved, let us love one another: for love is of God; and every one that loveth is born of God, and knoweth God." 1 John 4:7*

> *"And above all things have fervent charity among yourselves: for charity shall cover the multitude of sins." 1 Peter 4:8*

Chapter 13 of the book of 1 Corinthians can be called the book of love because it speaks entirely of charity, which is love. In 1 Corinthians 13, we find that love is not: boastful, rude, self-seeking, evil, envious, easily provoked, or proud. We find that in having charity, we are not seeking to harm or insult our neighbors; it does not rejoice in evil ways or deeds. And we note that true love never fails and abides forever.

Because God's love is perfect, we know that nothing can separate us from his love. And in Romans 8:38-39, the apostle Paul assures us of this fact:

> *"For I am persuaded, that neither death, nor life, nor angels, nor principalities, nor powers, nor things present, nor things to come, Nor height, nor depth, nor any other creature, shall be able to separate us from the love of God, which is in Christ Jesus our Lord." Romans 8:38-39*

We Are Assured of His Love

In the Bible, we are assured that nothing can separate us from God's perfect love, the love that sent Christ Jesus for us.

Love Is Not an Option

For us Christians, love is not an option; the Lord commands it.

> "A new commandment I give unto you, That ye love one another; as I have loved you, that ye also love one another. By this shall all men know that ye are my disciples, if ye have love one to another." John 13:34-35

In showing love to one another, we show the world that we are children of God. And when we live in love, we show that we do indeed follow his commandments.

> "And this is love, that we walk after his commandments. This is the commandment, That, as ye have heard from the beginning, ye should walk in it." 2 John 1:6

Love Is the Way

Love is the way to gain spiritual gifts such as prophecy, discernment, faith, and self-sacrifice. This we know by reading 1 Corinthians 13.

Love is the fulfillment of the law and the bond of perfection.

> *"Love worketh no ill to his neighbour: therefore love is the fulfilling of the law." Romans 13:10*
>
> *"And above all these things put on charity, which is the bond of perfectness." Colossians 3:14*

Jesus is the way, the truth, and the life, and his way is one of love. So follow that love as you live your life, and be perfected in all that you do.

"A new commandment I give unto you, That ye love one another; as I have loved you, that ye also love one another. By this shall all men know that ye are my disciples, if ye have love one to another." John 13:34-35

--- *Notes* ---

--- *Notes* ---

--- *Notes* ---

--- *Notes* ---

--- *Notes* ---

--- *Notes* ---

www.ingramcontent.com/pod-product-compliance
Lightning Source LLC
LaVergne TN
LVHW041539060526
838200LV00037B/1058